W9-CLW-005

FAMOUS NASCAR TRACKS

Jim Gigliotti

x1000r/min

CRABTREE PUBLISHING COMPANY

Crabtree Publishing Company

www.crabtreebooks.com

Coordinating editor
Chester Fisher

Series and project editor
Shoreline Publishing Group LLC

Author
Jim Gigliotti

Project Manager
Kavita Lad (Q2AMEDIA)

Art direction
Rahul Dhiman (Q2AMEDIA)

Design
Ranjan Singh (Q2AMEDIA)

Cover Design
Ravijot Singh (Q2AMEDIA)

Photo research
Anasuya Acharya & Amit Tigga (Q2AMEDIA)

Manuscript development and photo research
assistance provided by Shoreline Publishing
Group LLC, Santa Barbara, California

Acknowledgments

The publishers would like to thanks the following
for permission to reproduce photographs:

Associated Press: page 6; David Boe: page 26 (right);
    James P. Kerlin: page 7; Jim Tiller: page 8;
    Joanna Pinneo: page 23; Ric Feld: page 19;
    Terry Renna: page 9; Willis Glassgow: page 17
Capital Pictures: page 15
Focus on Sport/Getty Images: page 16
Joe Robbins: pages 4-5, 10-14, 18, 20-22, 24-25,
    26 (left), 28-29
Joe Williams, Bristol Motor Speedway, Bristol:
    cover and title page

Library and Archives Canada Cataloguing in Publication

Gigliotti, Jim
    Famous NASCAR tracks / Jim Gigliotti.

(NASCAR)
Includes index.
ISBN 978-0-7787-3188-7 (bound).--ISBN 978-0-7787-3196-2 (pbk.)

    1. NASCAR (Association)--Juvenile literature. 2. Stock car racing--United
States--Juvenile literature. 3. Racetracks (Automobile racing)--United
States--Juvenile literature. I. Title. II. Series: NASCAR (St. Catharines, Ont.)

GV1033.G53 2007   j796.7206'8   C2007-907257-7

Library of Congress Cataloging-in-Publication Data

Gigliotti, Jim.
    Famous NASCAR tracks / Jim Gigliotti.
       p. cm.
    Includes index.
    ISBN-13: 978-0-7787-3188-7 (rlb)
    ISBN-10: 0-7787-3188-X (rlb)
    ISBN-13: 978-0-7787-3196-2 (pb)
    ISBN-10: 0-7787-3196-0 (pb)
    1. Racetracks (Automobile racing)--United States--Juvenile literature. 2.
Stock car racing--United States--Juvenile literature. 3. NASCAR (Association)-
-Juvenile literature. I. Title.

    GV1033.G54 2008
    796.72--dc22
                                            2007048440

Crabtree Publishing Company

www.crabtreebooks.com   1-800-387-7650

Published in Canada
Crabtree Publishing
616 Welland Ave.
St. Catharines, ON
L2M 5V6

Published in the United States
Crabtree Publishing
PMB16A
350 Fifth Ave., Suite 3308
New York, NY 10118

Published in the United Kingdom
Crabtree Publishing
White Cross Mills
High Town, Lancaster
LA1 4XS

Published in Australia
Crabtree Publishing
386 Mt. Alexander Rd.
Ascot Vale (Melbourne)
VIC 3032

Contents

Track Stars

Drivers such as Jeff Gordon, Tony Stewart, and Dale Earnhardt Jr. aren't the only stars in NASCAR. Like famous stadiums such as baseball's Fenway Park and football's Lambeau Field, many stock car tracks are star attractions, too. These places boast a tradition that makes them a big part of NASCAR history.

More Than Meets the Eye

Ever see that television advertisement where the passenger in a delivery truck on a NASCAR track is giving directions to the driver? "Make a left here," he says. "Another left. Another left." It's a pretty funny commercial. But there's a lot more to driving around a NASCAR track than going around in circles. Besides, making all left turns won't work on a road course. But more about that later on!

The most famous "track star" on the NASCAR schedule is Daytona International Speedway.

Each One is Unique

Ladies and gentlemen, start your engines...It's race day at Daytona! More than 168,000 fans pack the Daytona International Speedway for the Daytona 500 each February—and that's just in the **grandstand**. Thousands more are on the **infield** or just soaking up the atmosphere in the nearby area. The fans come back again for the Pepsi 400 each July. Daytona is one of the most famous tracks in NASCAR. The excitement and pageantry of Daytona give it a personality all its own.

That's right, just as each NASCAR driver has his own unique personality, each track has its own personality, too—from the wild and free-wheeling tradition of Talladega to the bang-'em-up style of Bristol. In this book, we'll learn about the four different types of track on which NASCAR races are run: the superspeedways, the intermediate tracks, the short tracks, and the road courses. Plus, we'll look at the different types of "game" that drivers must bring to each type of track.

Bristol Motor Speedway gives stock car fans some of the season's most exciting racing.

The Great American Track

If the annual Daytona 500 is the "Great American Race," then the Daytona International Speedway should be called the "Great American Track." There's no doubt that Daytona is the biggest superstar among NASCAR tracks.

Daytona International Speedway

You don't even have to consider yourself a NASCAR fan to know that Daytona International Speedway is the most famous stock car racing track in the United States. It's the home of the Daytona 500. In addition to being known as the "Great American Race," the Daytona 500 sometimes is called the "Super Bowl of NASCAR." Whatever it's called, though, the Daytona 500 is NASCAR's most important race. It's the one that every driver dreams of winning.

That's Lee Petty (42) and Johnny Beauchamp (73) racing on the last lap of the 1959 Daytona 500. Petty won the race by just about the same margin that he held in this photo. The official winning margin is listed as two feet (0.3 m).

Late Winner

There have been lots of memorable races at Daytona, including the 2007 Daytona 500, when Kevin Harvick barely beat Mark Martin in a thrilling finish. But no Cup Series race may ever top the very first one at Daytona International Speedway. Lee Petty won the 1959 Daytona 500 in a race that is still remembered. That year, Petty's No. 42 car and Johnny Beauchamp's No. 73 car raced side by side in a furious chase to the finish line. They crossed the line at just about the same time. But so did another car. It was Joe Weatherly's No. 48 car. Weatherly was one lap behind, but he crossed on the high side between Petty, who was in the middle of the track, and the judges. They couldn't tell who won. At first, they said it was Beauchamp. He posed for pictures after the race with the trophy and Miss Daytona. But NASCAR quickly called the results unofficial, and began looking over pictures and film sent in from anyone who was at the race. Three days later, Petty was declared the official winner. Almost 50 years have passed since then, but Daytona's **inaugural** race still stands as one of the greatest in NASCAR history.

Man With a Plan

Daytona International Speedway was built in Daytona, Florida, in the late 1950s when NASCAR founder Bill France Sr. envisioned the Daytona 500 as the **premier** event on the schedule. Stock car races had been held on the hard-packed sands of Daytona for many years already. Drivers would compete on a track that took them from the beach to the city streets, then back to the beach again. Cars would pull into corners, kicking up sand at the spectators lined along the course. It was a lot of fun for everyone, and it made for some memorable race scenes. But France knew that if stock car racing was to grow into a national sport, it needed a **signature** race at a signature racetrack. In 1959, that dream was fulfilled when Daytona International Speedway opened, and the Daytona 500 was born. In 2008, the Daytona 500 was run for the 50th time.

Before the speedway was built, cars raced along a course that covered city streets and the beach.

Air Force One, with President George W. Bush aboard, takes off during the Daytona 500 in 2004. President Bush talked with drivers before the race and gave the starting call.

Of Presidents and Kings

The Daytona International Speedway is the number one racetrack in the country, and it's not just because of the Daytona 500. The 500 caps a week's worth of racing that also includes the annual Budweiser Shootout and the Gatorade Duels (unofficial events that don't count in the season standings). In fact, the two weeks leading up to the Daytona 500 are called "Speedweeks." In those two weeks, NASCAR drivers and their crews get their cars ready for action after the off-season. There are lots of different tests and qualifying races for cars and trucks in all NASCAR classes. Being at Daytona in those two weeks is a race fan's dream! Later in the year, the Pepsi 400 (previously known as the Firecracker 400) is held during the week of the Fourth of July. Richard "The King" Petty's

200th (and last) career victory came in the 1984 Firecracker 400 at Daytona, with President Ronald Reagan in attendance. President George W. Bush also attended a race at Daytona. He was at the Daytona 500 in 2004.

A Tri-Oval

Daytona International Speedway is a 2.5 mile (4 km) tri-oval racetrack. Except for the road courses of Watkins Glen International and Infineon Raceway, all NASCAR tracks are ovals. A few, however, are classified as "tri-ovals." That means that there's a "hump," or fifth turn, in the shape of the track. Daytona, Talladega Superspeedway, Pocono Raceway, Chicagoland Speedway, and Kansas Speedway are examples of tri-ovals.

Into the Draft

Naturally, speed is king at the superspeedways. Because the Daytona 500 comes at the beginning of the year, when all of the drivers are rested and the equipment is fresh, the race annually has rip-roaring action. The high-**banked** turns and long straightaways have something to do with that, too! Drivers also quickly learned the importance of **drafting** at a superspeedway such as Daytona. That's when one driver keeps his car close behind the bumper of the car in front of him. The laws of **aerodynamics** help the back car use less energy, but go faster than it normally would. Junior Johnson, a famous driver in the 1950s and 1960s, discovered the benefits of drafting at Daytona during qualifying for the 500 in 1960. He went on to win the race, and soon everyone was following his lead.

There's nothing quite like the experience of being at the Daytona 500—and that goes for the drivers on the track as well as the fans in the stands.

Speed Kings

The superspeedways are where race drivers can let it all hang out. These long tracks (two or more miles) have wild, full-throttle racing, three, and sometimes four, cars wide.

Talladega Superspeedway

At 2.66 miles (4.28 kilometers), Talladega Superspeedway in Talladega, Alabama, is the largest track on the NASCAR schedule. Its steep banks and wide straightaways mean some of the fastest—and most dangerous—racing on the circuit. The track is among the most popular with NASCAR fans for its history of exciting racing. A race at Talladega almost always has lots of lead changes, a sprint to the finish—and at least one large, high-speed wreck, too.

The racing at Talladega is fast and furious. Remember, the cars so close together in these photos are zooming along at 160 to 180 miles (257 to 290 km) per hour!

The Need for Speed

Drivers have reached as much as 220 miles (354 km) per hour down the straightaway at Talladega. Unfortunately, this also can lead to terrifying accidents. In fact, the day before the first NASCAR race there in 1969, drivers went on strike because they felt that the conditions were not safe. NASCAR went ahead with the race with replacement drivers after various safety experiments. In 1987, Bill Elliott set a NASCAR record when he averaged 212.809 miles (342.483 km) per hour during a qualifying run at Talladega. Ten years later, Mark Martin set another record for average speed during a race: 188.354 miles (303.126 km) per hour. Naturally, it came at Talladega, too.

Wild and Woolly

Talladega has been the home of some of the wildest races in NASCAR history. Imagine zooming along at nearly 200 miles (322 km) per hour with several other cars alongside, in front, and behind. In 1984, Cale Yarborough won the Winston 500 by two car lengths over Harry Gant. That capped a day on which the lead changed hands a record 75 times among 13 different drivers. In the summer of 2000, Dale Earnhardt Sr. won the Talladega 500 when he came back from 18th place with only five laps to go. At Talladega, like the old saying goes, "it's never over 'til it's over!"

You can see from this photo how steep the banks are in the turns at Talladega. That helps the cars maintain their blazing speeds.

Restrictor-Plate Racing

In response to increasing high speeds and sometimes unsafe conditions on the superspeedways, NASCAR began "restrictor-plate" racing at Talladega and Daytona in the late 1980s. With so many cars going so fast and driving so close together, the chance for a huge crash were too great. So NASCAR required cars to use the thin, metal plates with four holes in them. The plates restrict airflow from the **carburetor** to the engine, which reduces **horsepower**, and makes the car go slower. Of course, "slower" in this case is still pretty fast!

Indianapolis Motor Speedway

The Indianapolis Motor Speedway is a relative newcomer to the NASCAR scene. And yet, it is one of the most famous racing sites in America. Indianapolis, of course, is the home of the Indianapolis 500, the historic race on the Indycar circuit. In 1994, however, the track hosted a professional stock car race for the first time. Indianapolis is different from other superspeedways because it's a flat track. There is no banking in the straightaway, and it has a modest 9 degrees in the turns. Compare that with Talladega, which banks 16.5 degrees in the frontstretch and 33 degrees in the turns.

The Brickyard

The annual NASCAR race in Indianapolis is called the Allstate 400 at the Brickyard. "The Brickyard" is the nickname for the Indianapolis Motor Speedway. It comes from the street-paving bricks that used to cover the track. Bricks weren't the original track surface in 1909—that was crushed rocks and tar, which track officials quickly realized was a mistake. So they brought in lots and lots of bricks— 3.2 million of them! With **mortar** poured between them, the bricks became the track's new surface. As the bricks began to wear down, though, asphalt was poured over them at various spots on the track. Eventually, asphalt covered all but a three-foot (0.9 m) wide stretch of bricks at the start/finish line. That stretch is still there today. "Kissing the bricks" is a tradition for the race winner.

It's a tradition: The winner of the Brickyard 400 and his entire crew kiss the bricks at the start/finish line after the race.

And they're off! For the first time ever, stock cars took the track at the Indianapolis Motor Speedway in 1994.

Local Boy Makes Good

Jeff Gordon was born in California, but his family moved to Pittsboro, Indiana, when he was a teenager. Pittsboro is only about 20 miles (32 km) from Indianapolis. Gordon often drove by the Indianapolis Motor Speedway and dreamed of racing there one day. But when he became a NASCAR driver in the early 1990s, it looked as if that dream had died. In 1994, though, NASCAR began racing at the "Brickyard." Gordon's victory in the inaugural event was an emotional one for him. He's won it three times since.

Not Quite the Oldest

The Indianapolis Motor Speedway, which was built in 1909, is nearly 100 years old. (The first Indy 500 was held in 1911). There's only one older, continually run motor speedway in the country. That's the historic Milwaukee Mile in Milwaukee, Wisconsin.

The Heart of NASCAR

Much of the NASCAR schedule is run on medium-length tracks, which are called the intermediate tracks. The Lowe's Motor Speedway is an intermediate track located in North Carolina—right in the heart of NASCAR country.

They're crazy about racing in North Carolina, where NASCAR holds big events in the spring and fall.

Lowe's Motor Speedway

Lowe's Motor Speedway is located in Concord, North Carolina. That's not far from Charlotte, which is NASCAR's hometown. Most NASCAR teams have their headquarters nearby, too. Lowe's Motor Speedway annually hosts NASCAR's All-Star Challenge (which doesn't count in the points standings), the Coca-Cola 600 (the longest race on the NASCAR schedule), and the Bank of America 500.

On the Big Screen

Lowe's Motor Speedway used to be called the Charlotte Motor Speedway. The track may look familiar even to non-racing fans because it has been used many times in motion pictures, television, and music videos. Among the movies that have filmed racing sequences at Lowe's include *Days of Thunder*, which starred Tom Cruise as a racecar driver (1990); *Stroker Ace*, with Burt Reynolds (1983); and *Speedway*, with Elvis Presley (1968). More recently, country music star Tracy Lawrence filmed the video to his hit song "If the Good Die Young" there.

That's Tom Cruise in a picture from the 1990 motion picture Days of Thunder. The film is one of the most popular racing movies ever made.

More Than Any Other

The intermediates play a big role in determining the winner of NASCAR's Sprint Cup. That's because, simply, there are more intermediate tracks on the schedule than any other type of track. In 2007, for instance, five of the ten races in the "Chase for the Cup" were on intermediate tracks. Some of the newer intermediate tracks, like those in Las Vegas and Phoenix, have been **derided** sometimes as "cookie-cutter" tracks because they are not as unique as some of the longer and shorter courses. But success on the intermediate tracks has become necessary to becoming a NASCAR champion.

Not Big, Not Little

Intermediate tracks are more than one mile (1.6 km), but less than two miles (3.2 km), in length. Drivers must do well on tracks like Darlington and Atlanta if they want to win a season championship.

Darlington Raceway

Once the long-time home of the Southern 500 on Labor Day Weekend, Darlington still hosts the Dodge Challenger 500 in the spring each year. Located in Darlington, South Carolina, it's one of the most historic tracks on the stock car schedule—and one of the drivers' favorites. "You never forget your first love," Dale Earnhardt Sr. once said, "whether it's a high school sweetheart, a faithful old hunting dog, or a fickle racetrack in South Carolina with a contrary disposition."

Bill Elliott got his nickname—"Million Dollar Bill"—for the bonus he received after winning the Southern 500 in 1985.

The Tortoise and the Hare

In 1950, Darlington was the site of the first 500 mile (804 km) race in NASCAR **annals**. You know the story of the tortoise and the hare? The hare could run faster than anyone else, but the tortoise, tired of hearing about it, challenged him to a race. The hare sped past the tortoise right from the beginning, and figured that he had time for a rest. But the tortoise never stopped. While the hare was asleep, the tortoise reached the finish line. "Slow and steady wins the race!" he said. Well, Johnny Mantz won the 1950 race at Darlington with a car that was as slow as a tortoise compared to the hares of the other drivers. Mantz had the poorest qualifying time of any of the competitors—more than eight miles (12 km) per hour slower than the pole sitter. Mantz not only went on to win the race, but he also finished nine laps ahead of second-place Fireball Roberts. Mantz's secret? It was the tires. He knew that he needed tires that could hold up during a 500 mile (804 kilometer) race on asphalt. Other drivers were used to much shorter races on dirt tracks. They used the same tires that they used in those races. And they didn't hold up as long as Mantz's tires did. So while the faster cars continually had to stop for new sets of wheels, Mantz's slower car kept right on going!

A Crown Jewel

The Southern 500 quickly became one of the "Crown Jewels" of NASCAR. The others were the Daytona 500, the Winston 500, and the Coca-Cola 600. In 1985, Bill Elliott took home a $1 million bonus from a NASCAR **sponsor** when his victory in the Southern 500 was his third among the Crown Jewel races that year. The Southern 500 was held for more than half a century beginning in 1950. After the 2004 season, the race lost its place on the schedule as a result of NASCAR's legal dispute with the Texas Motor Speedway. Still, NASCAR visits Darlington once a year in the spring.

The harrowing trek up near the walls has given Darlington its nickname: "The Track Too Tough to Tame."

Fish Story

Darlington is unlike any other track in NASCAR. For one thing, the fastest way around it is to remain up near the walls—which leaves dents and marks on everyone's car by the end of the race (not to mention on the walls!). Plus, there's the shape. When the track was first built in the 1940s, a local landowner didn't want his minnow pond disturbed. So builders narrowed the west end of the track to accommodate the pond. The track wound up with an egg shape.

Atlanta Motor Speedway

The Atlanta Motor Speedway is one of the older tracks on the NASCAR circuit, but it looks a lot different than it did when it first opened in 1960. The track has undergone several renovations since then, including a new grandstand in 2006 that brought the seating capacity to 124,000 fans. Atlanta hosts two NASCAR races each year: the Kobalt Tools 500 early in the schedule and the Pep Boys Auto 500 in the fall.

Ticket to the White House

When the track opened in 1960 as the Atlanta International Raceway, it became just the seventh paved speedway of a mile or longer to host a NASCAR Cup Series race. Of those tracks, only Darlington, Daytona, and Lowe's (in addition to Atlanta) still are on the NASCAR schedule. Another bit of trivia: In the early 1960s, Jimmy Carter was a ticket man at the track. Carter soon was elected to the state **legislature** in Georgia, and he went on to become Governor of the state in 1970; in 1976, he was elected president of the United States.

The "Before" photo: The 2005 Bass Pro Shops MBNA 500 was held less than four months after the track was hit hard by a tornado. The speedway was repaired and the stands were packed come race day.

The "After" photo: Atlanta hosted a 500 mile (804 km) race in October, 2005.

Tornado Watch

In 2005, a tornado caused more than $10 million worth of damage to the track. The tornado had been **spawned** by Hurricane Cindy, which made landfall in Louisiana. Workers quickly began rebuilding the grandstand and other areas hit by the tornado. Less than four months later, the speedway still successfully hosted the Georgia 500.

For Dale Sr.

One of the most memorable days at the Atlanta Motor Speedway came in 2001. Just one month after Dale Earnhardt Sr. was killed in a last-lap crash at the Daytona 500, the speedway released thousands of black balloons on Lap 3 of the Cracker Barrel 500. At the same time, fans in the grandstand held up three fingers (Dale Sr. drove the No. 3 car). But things really got emotional when Kevin Harvick, the driver who took over for Earnhardt on the Richard Childress team, won the race.

Fan Favorite

A short track is, well...short! It is any track that is one mile (1.6 km) or less in length. The favorite short track among NASCAR fans is in Bristol, Tennessee, where drivers can't afford to give an inch in some of the fiercest "bang-'em-up" racing on the schedule.

Bristol Motor Speedway

One of NASCAR's most popular tracks, Bristol Motor Speedway, annually hosts two 500 mile (804 km) NASCAR races, the DirecTV 500 and the Sharpie 500. The racetrack was built on an old dairy farm in Tennessee, and it was modeled after Charlotte Motor Speedway (now called Lowe's Motor Speedway). In 1962, Bristol became the first wholly concrete track to host a NASCAR race.

You can see from this photo how the spectators are right on top of the racing action at Bristol.

Get Your Tickets Early

It's a short track, but Bristol boasts one of the largest seating capacities of any NASCAR track. When Bristol hosted its first NASCAR Cup Series race in 1961, it seated only 18,000 spectators. The track proved to be so popular with racing fans in the area, though, that seating was gradually increased, first to 71,000, then in increments up to its current level of 160,000. Even at that, though, a ticket to a nighttime race at Bristol in late summer is one of the hardest to get in NASCAR.

Volunteer Driver

Jack Smith officially is listed as the first winner of the Cup Series race at Bristol in 1961. But Smith wasn't the man behind the wheel when the No. 46 Pontiac crossed the finish line! Instead, it was Johnny Allen who was in the driver's seat at the checkered flag of the Volunteer 500. Smith began the race as the No. 46 driver, but then had to give way after 290 laps—that was allowed by NASCAR rules—because his feet were burned on the floorboard. Allen had begun the race in a different car, but he had to drop out when the car broke an **axle**. Forty-two cars started that race, but only 19 were running at the end.

The small track at Bristol makes for some close-knit racing—sometimes a little too close!

Old School

Short-track competition is the racing of choice for many traditional NASCAR fans. The smaller courses and lower speeds make for tighter quarters. That means bumper-to-bumper and door-to-door, get-out-of-my-way racing! Short-track racing also is closer to the sport's original roots. Early NASCAR races often were on dirt tracks of about one mile (1.6 km) or so in length.

Door-to-Door Racing

Drivers can't go blistering speeds on a short track—at some places, the winner averages fewer than 100 miles (161 km) per hour. But tracks like these in the South are really popular with racing fans.

Richmond International Raceway

Originally a dirt track from the early 1950s, Richmond International Raceway's oval is just three-quarters of a mile (1.2 km) long. The racing in such tight quarters makes it another NASCAR fan favorite. Richmond hosts two NASCAR races each season. The track in Richmond, Virginia, is a versatile **venue** that hosts lots of different events when NASCAR is not in town. In addition to trade shows and expos, it is the site of an annual Indy car race.

Last Call for the Playoffs

The second race at Richmond each year is the Chevy Rock & Roll 400. The race under the lights has long been a popular stop on the NASCAR schedule. But the event has taken on added significance in recent seasons because it has marked the cutoff for the "Chase for the Sprint Cup." In 2006, for instance, Kasey Kahne was on the outside of the playoffs looking in going into the Chevy Rock & Roll 400. A strong, third-place showing at Richmond, however, vaulted Kahne into the Chase.

The cars are a blur during nighttime action at Richmond. Every race at Richmond is under the lights.

Of course, it can work the other way, too. Tony Stewart won the 2005 season points championship and was in eighth place entering the Chevy Rock & Roll 400 the following season. But Stewart didn't get a chance to defend his title in the Chase when an 18th-place finish at Richmond dropped him to 11th overall (only 10 drivers made the Chase that year). In 2007, Dale Earnhardt Jr. needed a big finish to make the Chase. He finished 30th, though, and he fell short of the playoffs.

Kyle Petty got his first victory—and a kiss from his wife, Patti—in Victory Circle at Richmond in 1986.

Like Father, Like Son

Kyle Petty's dad, Richard Petty, won a record 200 NASCAR races, with the last coming in 1984. In 1986, Kyle was a 25-year-old looking for his first career NASCAR win. He got it at Richmond in the Miller High Life 400 in dramatic fashion. Late in the race, Darrell Waltrip and Dale Earnhardt Sr. were battling for the lead. The two legends crashed hard into the wall, however. Kyle Petty zoomed past and beat everyone else to the checkered flag.

Dover International Speedway

Almost all NASCAR tracks are asphalt. Dover is an exception. It's paved with concrete. That can be tough on a car's tires, and that's one reason that racing at Dover is such a challenge for any driver. Another reason: the track is narrow despite being a full one mile (1.6 km) in length. Winning at Dover International Speedway requires such driving skill that 21 of the first 22 champions there also won NASCAR season points titles at some stage of their careers. The brutal test that Dover provides helped the track earn the nickname "The Monster Mile." Dover hosts two NASCAR races each season, including one over the course of the "Chase for the Sprint Cup." The oval surrounds the Dover Downs horse track in Dover, Delaware.

American Pride

Dover was the site of the first NASCAR event held after the September 11 **terrorist** attacks on the United States in 2001. It was an emotional day at the track. Fans in the grandstands were given small American flags when they walked through the gates, and country music star Tanya Tucker sang patriotic songs. After the race, winning driver Dale Earnhardt Jr. circled the track waving a large American flag out the window of his No. 8 car. "I don't think it would have mattered who won this race," Dale Jr. said. "The fact that we're driving and racing and the fans can witness a good race is just healing enough."

Dale Earnhardt Jr. and Old Glory took an emotional victory ride together at Dover in 2001.

Martinsville Speedway

The Martinsville Speedway in Martinsville, Virginia, has been around even before NASCAR existed. Martinsville originally was a one mile (1.6 km) dirt track that opened in 1947. After NASCAR was formed in 1948, Martinsville hosted a race on the Fourth of July that year. The next year, NASCAR began running its "Strictly Stock" series (that's what has become the Sprint Cup today), and Martinsville was the sixth race on the schedule. Today, Martinsville is the only original NASCAR track still hosting Sprint Cup events.

Classic Course

In 60 years since it hosted its first NASCAR race, Martinsville's 0.526 mile (0.847 km) layout has not changed. The only difference is that the dirt track was converted to asphalt in the mid-1950s. One lap at Martinsville is the shortest lap in NASCAR.

There's not a lot of room to run at Martinsville. Tony Stewart (20) and Ryan Newman (12) show that the racing action can be door-to-door—

On the Road Again

What makes a road course different from any other NASCAR track? There are right turns! Remember that television commercial we talked about? Well, there's a lot more than just four left turns on a road course. A road course **emulates** racing on real streets.

With the countryside in the background, the setting at Watkins Glen is picture perfect.

Watkins Glen International

Watkins Glen (in New York) is one of the best-known road courses in the United States. It began as the dream of a law school student from Ohio whose family spent its summers vacationing in the area. His name was Cameron Argetsinger, and he wanted a place to race his sports car. So he designed a track on the asphalt, cement, and dirt roads of Watkins Glen. In 1948, the course hosted its first road race.

When Jeff Gordon (24) spun out in 2007, Tony Stewart (20) zoomed past and won the race.

Open Wheels, Too

Watkins Glen has hosted road racing of almost every different class since it first opened in the late 1940s. Most notably, it was the site of the United States Grand Prix for 20 years beginning in 1961. It has hosted a NASCAR Cup Series event each year since 1986. NASCAR's Busch Series and Craftsman Truck Series also have run races at "The Glen."

Keep Your Eyes on the Road

Seven of Watkins Glen's 11 turns are right-hand turns. That means that drivers need to really be on their toes all the time. Jeff Gordon was reminded of that the hard way in the Centurion Boats at the Glen in 2007—and Gordon is one of the best road-course drivers in the world. He was just a couple of laps from his record 10th Cup Series victory on a road course when he took a turn too fast and spun out. Gordon called the move "stupid," but knew it could happen to anyone. "That mistake is not a difficult one to make," Gordon said after finishing in ninth place. "That corner is ridiculously difficult…I'm just disappointed."

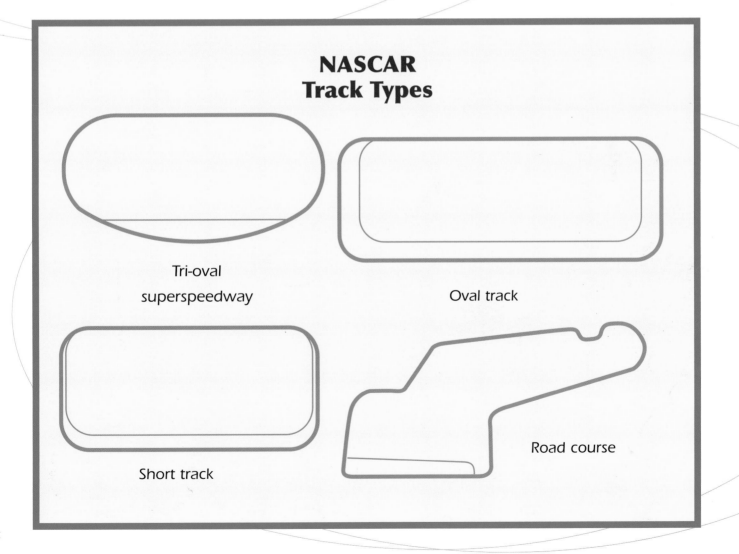

NASCAR Track Types

Tri-oval superspeedway

Oval track

Short track

Road course

Infineon Raceway

Infineon Raceway is a road course near Sonoma, California. It features a whole bunch of twists and turns to challenge a driver's ability. A driver has to negotiate 12 turns in all on the difficult track. Infineon might be the busiest racetrack in the country. It has hosted an annual NASCAR race each year since 1989. But it's also busy with on-track activity featuring all kinds of vehicles the entire year round. There's something going on at Infineon an average of 340 days a year.

Infineon Raceway is located in the heart of northern California's Wine Country in Sonoma, California.

Lost in Translation

The annual NASCAR race at Infineon is called the Dodge/Save Mart 350. But the race is only 110 laps around the 1.99 mile (3.2 km) course. How can it be a 350? That's because, unlike other NASCAR races, it's measured in kilometers, not miles. The race is just about 219 miles, or 352 kilometers. So maybe it really should be the Dodge/Save Mart 219!

The Great Debate

Should road courses be part of the Chase for the Sprint Cup? Right now, the events at both Watkins Glen and Infineon help drivers qualify for the Chase. But, since neither one is among the final 10 races of the year, the road courses don't factor into the playoffs. A lot of NASCAR fans think that a road-course race should be in the Chase, figuring that the Sprint Cup should reward the best all-around driver. But the other school of thought counters that NASCAR is a sport built on the ovals, and the Chase should be reserved for the races on those tracks. So far, that's the way NASCAR sees it, too.

Road Warriors

Tony Stewart won both of NASCAR's roadcourse events in 2007 (at Watkins Glen and Infineon). That gave him seven career victories on road courses, which is second only to Jeff Gordon on the all-time list. Gordon has won at Sonoma five times since 1998. Here are the drivers with the most NASCAR Cup Series wins on road courses.

Drivers	*Road Course Wins
Jeff Gordon	9
Tony Stewart	7
Bobby Allison	6
Richard Petty	6
Ricky Rudd	6
Rusty Wallace	6

*entering 2008

Here's a familiar sight: Jeff Gordon celebrated after winning at Sonoma for the fifth time in his career in 1998.

Facts and Figures

What's the longest? What's the shortest? Who are the best shorttrack drivers? Here are a few facts about NASCAR tracks...and the men who drive on them.

By Category

These are the different types of tracks on the NASCAR schedule:

Superspeedways

Daytona International Speedway

California Speedway

Indianapolis Motor Speedway

Michigan International Speedway

Pocono Raceway (Long Pond, Pennsylvania)

Talladega Superspeedway

Intermediate Tracks

Atlanta Motor Speedway

Chicagoland Speedway

Darlington Raceway

Homestead-Miami Speedway

Kansas Speedway

Kentucky Speedway

Las Vegas Motor Speedway

Lowe's Motor Speedway (Concord, North Carolina)

New Hampshire International Speedway

Texas Motor Speedway

Short Tracks

Bristol Motor Speedway

Dover International Speedway

Martinsville Speedway

Phoenix International Raceway

Richmond International Raceway

Road Courses

Infineon Raceway (Sonoma, California)

Watkins Glen

The Long and Short of It

NASCAR's longest race is the 600 mile (965 km) Coca-Cola 600 at Lowe's Motor Speedway. The shortest race is the 218.9 mile (352 km) Dodge/Save Mart 350 at Infineon Raceway.

These are the longest tracks on the NASCAR schedule.

Track	Length (one lap)
Talladega Superspeedway	2.66 miles (4.28 km)
Daytona International Speedway	2.5 miles (4 km)
Indianapolis Motor Speedway	2.5 miles (4 km)
Pocono Raceway	2.5 miles (4 km)

...and these are the shortest:

Track	Length (one lap)
Martinsville Speedway	0.526 miles (0.847 km)
Bristol Motor Speedway	0.533 miles (0.858 km)

Bank on It

For about 30 years or so, Bristol Motor Speedway has advertised itself as the NASCAR track with the steepest banks in the turns: 36 degrees. But Ryan Newman wasn't buying it. So several years ago, the driver of the No. 12 car, who has a degree in structural engineering from Purdue University, went out to measure the banks himself. He found that they were more like 26 degrees. Well, when Bristol was resurfaced in 2007, the workers discovered that Newman was right. Whether the track got worn down over the years or someone just made a mistake 30 years ago, Bristol no longer has the steepest banks. The new track measures out at about 30 degrees in the turns. That still makes it one of the tracks with the steepest banks on the NASCAR schedule. But it puts Bristol a little behind the superspeedways of Daytona and Talladega. These are now the NASCAR tracks with the steepest banks:

Track	Banks (Degrees)
Talladega	33
Daytona	31
Bristol	30
Darlington	*25
Atlanta	24
Dover	24
Lowe's	24
Texas	24

*Turns 1 and 2

Note: Indianapolis Motor Speedway is the flattest track, with just 9 degrees banking in the turns.

Super at the Superspeedway

"There's just no better place to win at than Daytona," says Jeff Gordon. He's had lots of experience at it. Gordon's six career victories at the track are tied for the third most of all-time. Here are the drivers with the most Cup Series wins at Daytona International Speedway:

Driver	*Victories
Richard Petty	10
Cale Yarborough	8
Bobby Allison	6
Jeff Gordon	6
David Pearson	6
Bill Elliott	4
Dale Jarrett	4
Fireball Roberts	4

*entering 2008; includes the Daytona 500 and the Pepsi 400

Best on the Short Tracks

Richard Petty is NASCAR's all-time leader with 200 career Cup Series victories. Not surprisingly, he's also No. 1 on the short tracks. Here are the all-time top five:

Driver	Short Track Wins
Richard Petty	139
David Pearson	52
Lee Petty	52
Ned Jarrett	48
Darrell Waltrip	47

Glossary

aerodynamics The motion of air and its effect on (in this case) racecars

annals Chronological records of events of succesive years

axle A long bar on which wheels turn

banked Sloped; the higher the degree of bank, the steeper the slope

carburetor A device used in an engine to produce an explosive mixture of vaporized fuel and air

derided Mocked, or laughed at

emulates Tries to be like

fickle Often changing in loyalty or affection

grandstand The place where spectators sit in seats or on benches

horsepower A unit of power

inaugural The first

infield The area inside the racing oval

legislature A body of people that have the power to make laws for a political unit

mortar A mixture of cement, sand, and water that hardens and binds together bricks or stones

premier The best

signature Distinguishing or identifying

sponsor A company that gives money to a person or team in exchange for promotion of the company's products or services

spawned Produced

terrorist A person who engages in an act of terrorism

venue The site of an event, usually a building

Index